Mental Health:
WE'VE ALL BEEN THERE:
Know it, understand it and squash it!

Epitoms

All rights reserved. No part of this publication may be reproduced, distributed, or transmitted in any form or by any means, including photocopying, recording, or other electronic or mechanical methods, without the prior written permission of the publisher, except in the case of brief quotations embodied in critical reviews and certain other noncommercial uses permitted by copyright law.

Copyright © Epitoms, 2022.

Table of contents

Chapter 1

Incase You Didn't Know

What is Mental Health?

Mental health comprises our emotional, psychological, and social well-being. It impacts how we think, feel, and behave. It also helps decide how we manage stress, react to others, and make good decisions.

Mental health is vital at every stage of life, from infancy and adolescence through maturity.

Although the phrases are sometimes used interchangeably, poor mental health and mental illness are not the same. A person might have poor mental health and not be diagnosed with a mental disease. Likewise, a person diagnosed with a mental illness might have times of physical, mental, and social well-being.

Why is Mental Health crucial for overall health?

Our mental well-being is as crucial as our existence itself.
Mental and physical health are equally vital components of total health. For example, depression raises the risk for many sorts of physical health issues, especially long-lasting illnesses like diabetes, heart disease, and stroke. Similarly, the existence of chronic illnesses might raise the risk for mental illness.

Can your Mental Health alter over time?

Yes, it's crucial to note that a person's mental health may fluctuate over time, depending on numerous things. When the pressures put on a person surpass their resources and coping skills, their mental health might be compromised. For example, if someone is working long hours, caring for a relative, or enduring economic difficulties, they may have poor mental health.

How prevalent are Mental illnesses?

Mental diseases are among the most frequent health issues in the United States.

More than 50% will be diagnosed with a mental disease or problem at some point in their lifespan.

1 in 5 Americans will encounter a mental illness in a given year.

1 in 5 children, either presently or at some time throughout their lives, have suffered a significantly debilitating mental disorder.

1 in 25 Americans lives with a significant
mental disease, such as schizophrenia,
bipolar disorder, or major depression.

Chapter 2

It Doesn't Just Happen!

What causes Mental illness?

There is no single cause for mental illness. Several factors can contribute to the risk of mental illness, such as

Early adverse life experiences, such as trauma or a history of abuse (for example, child abuse, sexual assault, witnessing violence, etc) (for example, child abuse, sexual assault, witnessing violence, etc.)

Experiences connected to other continuing (chronic) medical illnesses, such as cancer or diabetes

Biological causes or chemical abnormalities in the brain
Use of alcohol or drugs

Having emotions of loneliness or isolation

Mental health relates to cognitive, behavioral, and emotional well-being. It is all about how people think, feel, and act. People occasionally use the word "mental health" to denote the absence of mental disease.

Looking after mental health may protect a person's capacity to enjoy life. Doing this includes balancing life activities, obligations, and attempts to create psychological resilience.

Stress, despair, and anxiety may all influence mental health and interrupt a person's routine.

Although health professionals typically use the phrase mental health, experts understand that many psychological problems have physical underpinnings.

Mental health is a condition of mental well-being that helps individuals to deal with the demands of life, realize their strengths, study well and work effectively, and contribute to their society.

The WHO believes that mental health is "more than merely the absence of mental diseases or disabilities."

Peak mental health is not just about controlling active diseases but also looking after continuing well-being and enjoyment.

It also underlines that sustaining and repairing mental health is vital individually and at a community and societal level.

In the United States, the National Alliance on Mental Illness estimates that roughly 1 in 5 persons encounter mental health difficulties each year.

Mental health may impact everyday life, relationships, and physical health.

However, this relationship also works oppositely. Circumstances in people's life, interpersonal interactions, and physical factors might lead to mental ill health.

Risk factors for mental health issues

Everyone is at some risk of acquiring a mental health issue, regardless of age, sex, income, or race. In the U.S. and most of the industrialized world, mental diseases are one of the primary causes of disability.

Social and socioeconomic circumstances, traumatic childhood experiences, biological characteristics, and underlying medical disorders may all impact a person's mental health.

Many persons with a mental health illnesses have more than one ailment at a time.

It is crucial to highlight that good mental health relies on a delicate balance of circumstances and that various components may contribute to developing these diseases.

The following variables may lead to mental health disturbances.

Continuous social and economic pressure

Having poor financial resources or belonging to a disadvantaged or persecuted ethnic group might raise the risk of mental health issues.

A 2015 Iranian study

Trusted Source cites various socioeconomic reasons for mental health disorders, including poverty and living on the outskirts of a big city.

The researchers also described flexible *(modifiable)* and inflexible *(nonmodifiable)* factors that affect the availability and quality of mental health treatment for certain groups.

Modifiable variables for mental health issues include:

socioeconomic factors, such as whether a job is accessible in the local area,\occupation,\ a person's degree of social involvement,\education,\ housing quality,\, and gender.

Nonmodifiable elements include:

gender,\sage,\ethnicity,\nationality.

The researchers observed that being female elevated the chance of impaired mental health status by roughly 4 times. People with a "weak economic status" also scored highest for mental health issues in this survey.

Several types of research suggest that unfavorable childhood events such as child abuse, parental loss, parental separation, and parental sickness greatly impair a developing kid's mental and physical health.

One of the most well-known causes of mental disease is maltreatment. This might entail physical, sexual, emotional, or verbal abuse and can also include bullying or neglect. Abuse may occur in childhood or maturity. Unfortunately, it is all too prevalent. One in five women, one in six children, and one in twenty men will be victims of sexual abuse at some time in their life.

When abuse is experienced in childhood, it may have a severe and enduring impact on mental health. Children who are mistreated are more prone to acquire anxiety, depression, post-traumatic stress disorder, and other mental diseases. They may also be more inclined to resort to drug misuse as a form of self-medicating.

In maturity, abuse may also contribute to mental disease. Victims of domestic abuse, for example, are more prone to suffer from anxiety, sadness, and post-traumatic stress disorder. Substance misuse is also intimately connected to mental disease.

People who misuse drugs or alcohol are more prone to suffer from depression, anxiety, and other mental problems. The use of drugs is frequent among persons who are going through unpleasant situations which further encourages the cycle of addiction.

There are also correlations between childhood maltreatment and other unfavorable experiences and different mental diseases. These situations also render persons sensitive to post-traumatic stress disorder (PTSD).

Biological factors;

Mental Illness In The Family

Mental health difficulties are frequently viewed as belonging to the domain of psychology, however new research has demonstrated that genetics plays a substantial influence on many mental diseases. In fact, according to the National Institute of Mental Health, nearly 50% of all mental disease is caused by inherited genetic or biological factors.

This implies that if you have a blood family with a mental disease, you are more likely to get one yourself. Mental diseases tend to run in families, so it's not unexpected that heredity is a culprit. Some mental diseases having a high hereditary component include

depression, bipolar disorder, and OCD. While the specific processes causing these illnesses are still being researched, it is known that genetics plays a crucial influence in their development.
Of all, just because you have a family member with a mental disease does not indicate that you will surely get one yourself.

This is when environmental influences come into play. Although one might have a propensity for mental illness, it does not indicate that one will inevitably experience it. While certain environmental variables might raise the risk of mental illness, others can protect against it.

The NIMH believes that genetic family history may increase the chance

Trusted sources of mental health issue as certain genes and gene variations put a person at increased risk.

However, numerous additional variables contribute to the development of these illnesses.

Having a gene related to a mental health disease does not ensure that a condition will emerge. Likewise, those without associated genes or a family history of mental disease might nonetheless develop mental health concerns.

Chronic stress and mental health diseases such as depression and anxiety may develop owing to underlying physical health problems, such as cancer, diabetes, and chronic pain.

Experiencing Discrimination and Stigma

People who have suffered prejudice or stigma are more prone to mental health difficulties. This is particularly true for groups that endure systematic discrimination, such as minority groups, people of color, the LGBTQIA+ community, and individuals with disabilities. Discrimination may take various forms, from microaggression to full-blown hate crimes. It can be overt or covert, intentional or unintentional. Regardless of its form, prejudice may have a major influence on mental health.

When people encounter prejudice, it may lead to feelings of humiliation, worthlessness, and loneliness. This may in turn develop into a mental health issue such as anxiety, depressive episodes, and post-traumatic stress disorder. It can also trigger or worsen existing mental health conditions. In rare situations, it may even lead to suicide.

The Loss Of A Loved One

The loss of a loved one is one of the most traumatic things a person can go through.

It's normal to experience sorrow, sadness, and rage when someone dear to you dies. However, for some people, these emotions can become so intense that they develop depression or anxiety.

In certain situations, the loss of a loved one might be abrupt and unexpected. This may make it even more difficult to handle. Sudden deaths may lead to emotions of shock and disorientation, which can be quite unpleasant. Loved ones are typically people who give our life meaning and purpose. So when they're gone, it might be hard to find a cause to keep going.

Moreover, the loss of a loved one may lead to emotions of isolation and loneliness. This is particularly true if the individual was a close friend or family member. When someone dies, it might seem like a part of you has died with them. This might make it hard to connect with other people and can create a vicious cycle of isolation and mental illness.

Trauma

All forms of traumatic events may lead to a mental health issue including war, natural disasters, rape/sexual assault, physical assault, bullying, neglect, and having a history of abuse or violent life situations. Trauma may have a dramatic influence on mental health. It may lead to symptoms such as post-traumatic stress disorder, flashbacks, nightmares, anxiety, and serious depression. Trauma may also make it difficult to trust other people, which can lead to social isolation.

Some people who have experienced trauma may also develop substance abuse problems as a way to cope with their pain. This may further worsen the condition and lead to a downward cycle of mental illness and addiction.

Traumatic occurrences don't necessarily need to be the massive, life-altering ones that we often think of. Sometimes, it might be the accumulation of minor, everyday life traumas that have a substantial influence on our mental health. This is particularly true for disadvantaged populations that endure many types of prejudice and violence.

Other causes that might induce mental illness are:

Mental health disorders may have a broad variety of causes. It's possible that for many individuals there is a complex blend of circumstances - however various people may be more profoundly influenced by some things than others.

For example, the following causes might result to poor mental health: childhood maltreatment, trauma, neglect\social isolation, or

loneliness\experiencing prejudice and
stigma, especially racism
social disadvantage, poverty or
debt\bereavement (losing someone dear to
you)
severe or long-term stress\shaving a
long-term physical health
condition\unemployment or losing your job
homelessness or bad housing
being a long-term caring for someone
drug and alcohol misuse\domestic violence,
bullying, or other abuse as an
adult\significant trauma as an adult, such as
military combat, being involved in a serious
incident in which you feared for your life, or
being the victim of a violent crime\physical
causes – for example, a head injury or a
neurological condition such as epilepsy can
have an impact on your behavior and mood.

(It's vital to rule out any physical reasons
before seeking additional therapy for a
mental health condition).

Although lifestyle issues such as job, nutrition, drugs, and lack of sleep may all impact your mental health, if you encounter a mental health problem there are frequently additional causes as well.

"My depression seems to flare up during times when I am stressed and isolated from other people."

Symptoms

Signs and symptoms of mental illness may vary, depending on the diagnosis, circumstances, and other variables. Mental disease symptoms may alter emotions, ideas, and actions.

Examples of signs and symptoms include:

Feeling melancholy or dejected.

Confused thinking or diminished ability to focus.

Excessive anxieties or worries, or severe emotions of guilt.

Extreme mood fluctuations of highs and lows.

Withdrawal from friends and hobbies.

Significant weariness, poor energy, or trouble sleeping.

Detachment from reality (delusions), paranoia, or hallucinations.

Inability to deal with everyday challenges or stress.

Trouble comprehending and connecting to circumstances and people.

Problems with alcohol or drug usage.

Major changes in dietary habits.

Sex urge changes.

Excessive wrath, antagonism, or violence.

Suicidal thought.

Chapter 3

The Toll On 'Us'

The World Health Organization (WHO) emphasizes the significance of psychological well-being, describing health as "a condition of full physical, mental and social well-being and not only the absence of sickness or infirmity". In 2018, of the estimated 792 million people worldwide living with a mental or behavioral disorder (roughly 10.7% of the global population), 178 million were drug or alcohol-dependent, 20 million were diagnosed with schizophrenia, and 264 million suffered from depression.

Though most efforts to improve global mental health focus on improving care for individuals living with psychological disorders, the WHO stresses that a comprehensive definition of mental health should extend beyond the absence or presence of diagnosable psychological disorders to include "subjective well-being, perceived self-efficacy, autonomy, competence, intergenerational dependence and recognition of the ability to realize one's intellectual and emotional potential". Although the next modules will concentrate on the public health consequences of psychological diseases, mental health delivery systems should leverage this more broad concept of mental health.

While it is often overlooked as a public health issue due to a historical focus on communicable and more immediately life-threatening diseases (such as HIV/AIDS and malaria), mental health has profound effects on an individual's quality of life, physical and social well-being, and economic productivity.

Because psychological disorders also affect families and communities of the mentally ill, understanding the effects of mental illness on individual patients and social systems is necessary for the improvement of mental health care systems and the development of effective mental health care delivery programs.

Effects of Psychological Disorders on the Patient

Individuals with psychiatric illnesses are at increased risk for diminished quality of life, educational challenges, lowered productivity and poverty, social issues, susceptibility to abuse, and extra health problems.

School is sometimes damaged when early-onset mental illnesses hinder persons from finishing their education or effectively pursuing a job. Kessler et al. (1995) observed that persons with psychiatric problems were much less likely to finish high school, join college, or get a college degree, compared to their counterparts without mental diseases.

In addition, psychiatric problems result in lost individual production owing to unemployment, missed work, and reduced productivity at work.

A 2001 research revealed that five to six million U.S. employees aged 16 to 54 years "lose, fail to seek, or cannot obtain employment" owing to mental illness. Of mentally ill persons who were working, mental illness was predicted to diminish their yearly income by $3,500 to $6,000.

Reduced wages and diminished work possibilities put mentally ill persons at an increased risk of poverty. As Lund et al. (2011) explain, mental illness and poverty "interact in a negative cycle", in which poverty functions as a risk factor for mental illness, and mental illness raises the probability that people would "drift into or stay in poverty".

This negative cycle may also contribute to high rates of homelessness among individuals with mental illness; the Substance Abuse and Mental Health Services Administration estimates that 20 to 25 % of the U.S. homeless population suffers from severe mental illness, while only 6% of the general U.S. population is severely mentally ill.

Psychological illnesses may also lead to other health issues and pressures. For instance, people with comorbid depression (depression co-occurring with another health condition) are three times less likely to adhere to medical treatment regimens than non-depressed patients.

Furthermore, mentally ill persons are susceptible to low-quality treatment, abuse, and human rights abuses, especially in low-income communities with minimal mental health care resources. Mentally ill persons and their families may also endure substantial societal stigma and prejudice.

Effects of Psychological Disorders on Families

The responsibility of caring for a mentally ill person generally falls on the patient's close family or relatives. Families and caregivers of persons with psychiatric problems are frequently unable to work at full capacity owing to the responsibilities of caring for a mentally ill individual, resulting in lower economic productivity and a drop in family income.

Loss of income and the financial demands of caring for a mentally ill individual placed these families at an elevated risk of poverty. Family members may also feel considerable and chronic stress owing to the emotional and physical demands of caring for a mentally ill family member.

Family members of mentally ill persons are confronted with a substantial degree of emotional upheaval; parents are challenged with readjusting parenting techniques and expectations, while partners must exhibit a considerable amount of patience and empathy to give proper care.
These obligations may weigh heavily upon the family members, depending on individual experience and culture, and must be given equal priority when evaluating the lingering impacts of mental illness on society.

For instance, a 2006 research in Botswana studied the experiences of families caring for a mentally sick family member. The research was done utilizing in-depth interviews, focus group talks, and field observations in Gaborone, the capital city, and Molepolole, a rural town.

Although the extended family structure typical in Botswana allowed for sharing of caregiver tasks, most families indicated that lack of financial and medical resources at the family and community levels made it difficult and stressful to provide proper care.

Effects of Psychological Disorders on Society

Although the precise socioeconomic effect of mental illness differs throughout cultures and countries, untreated mental illness has enormous costs to society. In 2001, the WHO projected that mental health disorders cost industrialized economies between three and four % of their GNP (gross national product) (gross national product). A 2018 Lancet Commission study on mental health has said that mental diseases are on the increase in every nation in the globe and would cost the global economy an estimated $16 trillion by 2030.

The economic impact is mostly due to the early onset of mental disease and lost productivity, with an estimated 12 billion working days lost due to mental illness per year. In 1997, a Harvard Medical School research projected that the United States missed more than 4 million workdays and had 20 million "work cutback days" (days of decreased job performance) owing to mental illness.

In addition, psychological problems may worsen other public health difficulties, increasing the strain on national economies and hampering international public health initiatives.

According to a 2020 WHO estimate, over 13 million individuals inject drugs worldwide, and 1.7 million of them are living with HIV. Injecting drug use accounts for approximately 10% of HIV infections globally and 30% of that outside of Africa.

Regional HIV prevalence rates are high among persons who inject drugs in all areas of the globe (up to 15.5% in East and Southern Africa).

People who utilize narcotics are also disproportionately impacted by hepatitis C. The estimated worldwide prevalence of hepatitis C in those who inject drugs is 67%. Further, globally there are roughly 2.2 million HIV–hepatitis C virus co-infections of which more than half are in persons who inject drugs.

Mental diseases are also related to a greater risk of non-adherence to medication regimens for other health issues. For infectious disorders, incorrect or insufficient use of a treatment may develop into drug resistance, which may have "profound public health implications" for the global society. Furthermore, maternal depression may put babies at higher risk of low birth weight, childhood health issues, and "incomplete immunization", all of which are risk factors for childhood death.

Although the majority of persons with mental illness do not display violent behaviors, violence and imprisonment among mentally ill individuals may inflict a huge financial and social burden on communities and countries.

Worldwide, nearly 10 million people are jailed, and the WHO states that the incidence of mental health disorders is "very high", particularly among female convicts. In the U.S. in the late 2000s, almost one million individuals with major psychiatric problems were jailed yearly.

A study in the Pinellas Country, Florida jail found that not having outpatient mental health treatment was significantly associated with an increased risk of misdemeanor arrests and days incarcerated, and having a substance abuse disorder was associated with more days in jail, which is consistent with national incarceration statistics.

National data from the 2002 Survey of Inmates in Local Jails revealed that homelessness was significantly more prevalent among the inmate population as compared to the general U.S. adult population, and inmates who had been homeless were significantly more likely than other inmates to have mental health and substance abuse problems.

The authors posit that the relationship between homelessness and mental illness "may reflect limited access to mental health services, particularly inpatient services", due to deinstitutionalization in the United States, which has resulted in limited availability of psychiatric hospital beds, and strict criteria for hospitalization.

The WHO recommends that developing and developed nations adopt more comprehensive preventative and interventional mental health programs to

reduce the negative effects of mental illness
on patients and their local and global
communities.

Chapter 4

The New 'Mindlook'

Mental health is a complicated topic with many distinct underlying risk factors. What they all have in common is that they may lead to feelings of loneliness, worthlessness, and despair. If you or someone you love is battling with mental illness, it's vital to know and realize that it's not the end of **YOU**.

There are various resources accessible to individuals that need help. With the correct assistance, mental illness may be controlled and individuals can have happy and healthy lives.

Chapter 5

Squash It!!!

Try these ways to retain your equilibrium, or re-balance yourself.

Value yourself:
Treat yourself with care and respect and avoid self-criticism. Make time for your hobbies and favorite endeavors, or widen your horizons. Do a daily crossword puzzle, grow a garden, take dancing classes, learn to play an instrument, or become proficient in another language.

Take care of your body:
Taking care of oneself physically may boost your mental wellness. Be sure to:

Eat healthful meals.

Avoid smoking and vaping.

Drink lots of water

Exercise helps lessen melancholy and anxiety and enhances spirits.

Get adequate sleep:
Researchers think that lack of sleep correlates to a high risk of depression among college students.

Surround yourself with excellent people:
People with strong familial or social ties are often healthier than those who lack a support network. Make arrangements with supportive family members and friends, or seek out activities where you may meet new people, such as a club, class, or support group.

Give yourself:
Volunteer your time and efforts to assist someone else. You'll feel good about doing

something concrete to assist someone in need — plus it's a fantastic opportunity to meet new people.

Learn how to cope with stress:
Like it or not, stress is a part of life. Practice healthy coping skills: Try One-Minute Stress Strategies, practice Tai Chi, exercise, take a nature walk, play with your pet or try journal writing as a stress reliever. Also, remember to smile and recognize the comedy in life. Research reveals that laughing may enhance your immune system, alleviate pain, relax your body and decrease stress.

Quiet your mind:
Try meditation, Mindfulness, and/or prayer. Relaxation techniques and prayer may enhance your state of mind and view on life. Research suggests that meditation may help you feel peaceful and boost the results of treatment.

Set realistic objectives:
Decide what you want to accomplish academically, professionally, and personally, and write down the actions you need to attain your goals. Aim high, but be realistic, and don't over-schedule. You'll have a fantastic feeling of satisfaction and self-worth as you work toward your objective.

Break up the monotony:
Although our routines make us more efficient and boost our emotions of comfort and safety, a little change of pace may brighten up a monotonous schedule. Alter your running routine, organize a road trip, take a stroll in a different park, hang some new photos or try a new restaurant.

Avoid alcohol and other drugs:
Keep alcohol use to a minimum and avoid other drugs. Sometimes individuals use alcohol and other drugs to "self-medicate"

yet in fact, alcohol and other drugs simply intensify issues.

Get assistance when you need it:
Seeking aid is a sign of strength — not a weakness. And it is crucial to remember that therapy is successful. People who seek adequate treatment may recover from mental illness and addiction and have full, meaningful lives.
Try all methods given above until you can firmly declare 'I crushed it!!!'

I AWAIT YOUR REVIEW.

www.ingramcontent.com/pod-product-compliance
Lightning Source LLC
Chambersburg PA
CBHW060921130726
48001CB00006B/2345